The Involved Parent

Tips for a Greater Connection with Your Child

ALRICK DOUGLAS, MA

Alrick Douglas, MA Paterson, New Jersey

Copyright © 2019 Alrick Douglas. All rights reserved. No part of this publication may be reproduced, stored in or introduced into a retrieval system, or transmitted, in any form or by any means (electronic, mechanical, photocopying, recording or otherwise), without the prior written permission of the copyright owner.

The scanning, uploading, and distribution of this book via the Internet or any other means without the authorization of the publisher are illegal and punishable by law. Please purchase only authorized electronic editions and do not participate in or encourage electronic piracy of copyrighted materials. Your support of the author's rights is appreciated.

Limits of Liability ~ Disclaimer

The author and publisher shall not be liable for your misuse of this material. This book is strictly for informational and educational purposes. The author and publisher do not guarantee that anyone following these techniques, suggestions, tips, ideas, or strategies will become successful. The author and publisher shall have neither liability nor responsibility to anyone concerning any loss or damage caused, or alleged to be caused, directly or indirectly by the information contained in this book.

Cover Design – Okomota

Editing-Interior Layout – The Self-Publishing Maven and The Edit Bae

Formatting – Rasel Khondokar

ISBN: 978-1-7334310-0-2

Printed in the United States of America

DEDICATION

I dedicate this book to my wife Candice and my daughters Aryana and Maigan. Their presence in my life enables me to live the truth of *The Involved Parent.*

ACKNOWLEDGMENTS

I am grateful to all the youths and their parents who I have worked with over my professional career as a counselor. The openness and honesty they displayed in communicating their challenges and need for therapeutic support, motivated me to prepare this tool so others can benefit and experience whole lives.

I also want to thank my mom and dad for appreciating, validating, and supporting my efforts for having a heart for people since my teenage years. Their house became a safe space where young people could easily come and be fed physically and emotionally.

I want to appreciate Rajae Powis and Malik Smith for sharing their stories in my capacity as their mentor. Their stories inspired this book in many ways. Additionally, this book could not have been in your hands today had it not been for my personal coach Dr. Jonathan Shaw, who challenges me every day to be consistent where I am passionate. I am forever motivated by his personal discipline and commitment to changing lives.

Table of Contents

Introduction 1

1. The Presenting Problem 5
2. Do You Know Me? 14
3. The Struggle Is Real 21
4. The "Wow" Moment 29
5. The Healthy Talk 34
6. Words are Arrows 44
7. The Honor Code 50
8. How to Be More Present 58
9. What Box Are You In? 65
10. Pulling It Together 70
11. Conclusion 74

Introduction

My inspiration to engage families and offer tips to improve relationship with their teens evolved from my experience mentoring youths over the years. The support needed was immense and I could not ignore their stories as they navigate hope in an environment that did not believe in their purpose or fuel their vision. I always desired to start a conversation on a local level that would generate public change. *The Involved Parent* provides important tips with real-life accounts of teenagers and their families to explain the need for parents to be more involved in their children's lives. Unfortunately, we do not live in a perfect world, and as a counselor, my goal is to help people who are in imperfect places, bringing them to a place of normalcy to benefit the social and emotional development of the child.

Parents have a voice in the conversation about unexpected events that shift what worked perfectly and creates an imbalance in how the family unit operates. It is important that dialogue be open with the parent and child, so there can be a more authentic relationship as sometimes a child will change their behavior when they hear from their parents that they are really being impacted. *The Involved Parent* provides tips for parents to be more vocal and open about their challenges to their child. Sometimes parents deem being open as weakness and they miss out on an opportunity to build a stronger relationship with their child. In some cases, their child's behavior can be a reflection of their inability to reconcile their uncertainty as to how their parent reacted to them.

I have always been passionate about impacting this generation with wisdom, strength, and healing so individuals can find the courage to lead whole lives and experience permanent change. Mentoring and coaching with teens for over 14 years has given me access to material on the challenges they experience within their homes and how they struggle to resolve issues with parenting. In my current capacity as Prevention of Juvenile Delinquency Counselor, I work extensively with high school students and their families to support the reunification process and avert students from having a juvenile record.

The Involved Parent provides tips on how to handle conversations in a manner that creates unity, builds a supportive environment and validates efforts towards change. These tips will prove effective if parents use them consistently when working with their children. The tips and strategies provide a level of support to parents as their child develops. These tools help engagement by not creating distance but by building a stronger connection and bond. This is critical as sometimes when parents overreach, the child pulls back because they were not ready to engage their parents about their issues. Additionally, parents must find the balance in giving their child space, and at the same time not neglect their need for support. This tool offers tips on how to engage a disengaged child.

This book captures real-life case studies of actual clients (names changed for confidentiality) who are experiencing the benefits of having an involved parent, or the deficit of a parent being absent. The goal here is to bring to perspective the benefits of the involved parent and how lives are impacted when parents are not present. Some of the case studies are success stories while others are parents being honest that the struggle is real and that support is not always present in the environment.

Working with students and families from various backgrounds increase my ability to see family values through their cultural lens. This mindfulness has transformed the lives of the students and their families tremendously. I've learned through my work that each family has different values that are culturally driven and must be validated before any attempt is made to modify them to meet the needs of the child. My ability to connect with my clients regardless of culture is what makes my work so transforming and impactful with today's youth.

I currently hold a Master's Degree in Counseling (Summa Cum Laude) and Bachelors of Arts in Language and Communication (Honors). These academic journeys have prepared me extensively for leading today's youth and their families, fostering personal growth and development. While mentoring teens, I garnered five years of experience as an in-home therapist, working with families who have children diagnosed with autism. This experience allowed me to see how a diagnosis can shift the core of a family structure, not taking into consideration one's social status.

As a parent with a hectic professional schedule, I have infused in this book tools I utilize to remain present in the life of my daughters as they develop; I too, can also relate to the challenges. I have seen first-hand how being present builds their social and emotional selves. I have also consulted the experiences of other parents and clients who both have success and challenges being an involved parent. This book is designed to open the conversation on how, as parents, we can be more present and engaging to our children as they navigate their personal journey to adulthood.

The Presenting Problem

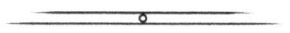

When a child is conceived, uncertainty may arise for those involved in the life changing journey. The mother becomes the carrier of an experience that ultimately alters her emotions, physical appearance, and social engagements. The father moves into preparation mode to support the mother's changes while dealing with the financial planning for the newborn. No matter how many commitments are made, or support offered, there is an aloneness that new parents experience. In the midst of this anticipation, both parents work tirelessly to ensure their newborn is in a safe and nurturing environment.

This is what the perfect life looks like when parents take responsibility for the seed they have planted and plan together to ensure it germinates and bear fruits. Sounds good right? Without acceptance and commitment to the responsibility of developing and nurturing a child, a parent becomes absent. There are instances where a parent will make a choice to transfer responsibility of their child's development to another person because they lack the resources to provide the life they think the child deserves. This book will focus on the essential question of what do you do when as a parent you feel disconnected from your child and how to reconnect those broken pieces to make the relationship whole and functional.

My interest in the absent parent/child phenomenon began during my professional experience as a counselor where I started as an intern in a middle school, and now working with the juvenile population in the high school. As a counselor, I am in a preventative role. I work closely with the police department and the school administration to pride psychoeducation to at risk students. These students who are not at risk are equally served to ensure they have all the tools needed to make decisions that would keep them out of the juvenile justice system. These roles afforded me the opportunity to counsel students from all levels of the social strata. One common denominator I found with children who lacked social and emotional development was that they were coping with an absent parent. It did not matter the racial or ethnic background of the students—there was a greater need for the missing parent. I spent hours listening to the cries of those students who were emotionally forced to choose which parent to love, to end the battle of daily choosing which parent is better. Others reported that switching houses was painful as they were not able to return home with any of the excitement they experienced while at mom or dad's home. The dysfunction that the absent parent phenomenon causes, cripples the child's deeper need for connectedness and oneness between both parents and affects their freedom to love both parents openly. No child should be placed in a position of choosing which parent to love. Sometimes parents ignore the benefits of not triangulating their children in the brokenness of their relationship. A greater care must be made so the emotional development of that child is preserved.

    The resistance to assistance is a common barrier that strengthens the negative effects of the absent parent. While serving the community, I would often mentor young men who were afraid to receive the assistance offered through my mentorship. It was not because they felt unsafe; it was their fear of what their parent would say if they received outside help. One mentee told me about the effects my mentorship had on his dad. His dad was hardly home due a hectic work schedule, which is common in a single parent household. Sometimes the absent parent develops an insecurity and pride, which translates to their children and blocks the assistance that is needed in the environment.

Additionally, absentee parenting breeds an environment where the child who lacks sufficient parental nurturing has the potential of experiencing a developmental crisis when they explore relationships. American-German psychologist Erik Erikson, describes this developmental stage as identity versus role development. The adolescent students I encounter in my daily work are directly experiencing the impact of the absent parent and struggle with identity and role development. As they begin to explore a greater sense of self and learn about their role as an adult, the pain and emotional deficit they have already experienced creates stagnation. Instead of focusing on their goals and future, they focus more on trying to resolve or even block the relationship with their absentee parent. They become trapped in a system that focuses more on resolving the need for the absent parent or coping with the choice they have to make of blocking their emotions to focus on their developing self. This failure to resolve the unfinished business can resurrect itself in later years.

There are success stories of children who have a strong resilience and emerge from these experiences unscathed. However, what remains uncertain is how they handle future relationships and life disappointments. I have had students who relapse in their adult years. Although they survived their adolescence coping with the absent parent, when they emerge into adulthood the trauma from the unfinished business of their earlier years resurfaces in other ways. The purpose of this book is not to turn a blind eye to the fact that some relationships require necessary ending for emotional well-being and safety. However, the impact on the child cannot go unnoticed and must become a guiding light when relationships come to an end. If as a single parent your load is heavy, seek out those community support programs that will assist in the development and maturity of your child. As you read the pages of this book, you will discover more of what the absent child is saying in their pursuit for professional help. I meet them in my office daily.

It must be noted that the absentee parent does not apply only to single parents. I've encountered many students who had both parents living in their house but were still absent. Some of these students had dual career parents who were hardly home due to hectic work schedules or business travels. I also served students, who had one parent in the house compromised by a diagnosis or mental health challenge. What I found noteworthy was the resiliency of these students; some found their own unique strategy to cope with the absent parent even though they wish the condition was otherwise.

An absent parent can stem from the result of death and the child grows up with the knowledge that they will never be in touch with the biological parent lost. I recently worked with a client whose father died before she was born. She was privately angry with her mom for not explaining to her what her father was like. This client shared that although she is coping better with the absence of her father, she just wanted to know more about his personality, if he was excited about her conception and who he was to her mom. She conveyed that her mom withheld the information as she was dealing with the pain of his death and how their relationship struggled. The client stated that her mom never wanted to entertain any conversation about her dad.

Parents should seek help from professionals if they are unable to communicate to their child the circumstances beyond the absence of the other parent. If the child desires to have a connection with the absent parent, it should be embraced. The opposite of such reality is a child developing with insecurities and low self-esteem or increased anger because of the unresolved absence of their parent.

As teens develop, some naturally grow apart from their parents. This shift from dependency to independence is often misinterpreted by parents as they deem the emerging adult as being non-compliant and disrespectful. However, what the child is communicating is a deeper need for support on how to navigate this inevitable journey as an adult and though your opinions may seem rejected, your child is listening. When parents are not supportive in helping their child navigate this important journey, it can potentially create a disconnect between parent and child.

Parents, your good intentions for your child is not going unnoticed. Parents who are successful in helping their children navigate this journey adapted a mindset of allowing their teens to learn from the mistakes of others or from their own. This atmosphere sees parents being supportive and restorative—creating an environment where the child can comfortably expose their error and get guidance. The absent parent absent child phenomenon is not a single parent crisis. It's a bigger conversation about how, as parents, the gap between you and your child can be reduced so they inherit the functional skills and help for their future needs.

Notes to Parent

- Your child may not communicate to you how they feel, so periodical check-ins are necessary.
- If separation is imminent and the child is mature enough to handle the conversation, avoid the surprise, sit down prior to the imminent change, and have a talk.
- Never force your child to choose who to love.

Do You Know Me?

When I sit with the students I meet daily and explore the connection they have with their parents, I hear one common complaint: "They don't know me." From a professional perspective, the average parent would deem this child to be ungrateful for all they have done to provide for their well-being. However, the students I see are not ungrateful or unappreciative of the efforts of their parents; they are reporting that the absence of one parent puts a strain on the other, resulting in excessive work schedule, emotional detachment, hard to unwind, etc. for the parent they live with. Children generally desire happiness and having a sense of comfort and stability. They rely on their parent's support to shield them from hardships and provide emotional steadiness. It's the parent's responsibility to meet those behind the scene needs. When they experience a breakdown in the family unit, social and emotional development is compromised and distracts the child's focus to the unresolved issues. When parents become distant from their children to cope with the internal struggles within the family unit, they leave an empty place that needs to be filled. What tends to happen is the child, in an attempt to self-regulate their emotions, resort to delinquent behaviors as they search for satisfaction. Know that the struggle is real and you are not being asked to abandon your true feelings about your situation. However, you cannot leave a child with an under-developed brain to formulate the appropriate response to social and emotional issues. As the role model, you will need to seek out strategies to compartmentalize your emotions, as you seek healing, so it does not put a strain on your child's development.

Your children are looking for a safe and nurturing environment to communicate their fears, insecurities and general mental health challenges. One common denominator of children I have worked with in the past is that they deem it pointless communicating with their parents. These students report experiencing a huge disconnect in how they perceive the world and their issues than that of their parents. This disconnect creates a sense of loneliness leaving the child vulnerable to peer support that could be ill-informed and misdirected. These responses speak to a greater work that must be done to ensure parents are spending quality time listening to the needs of their children. It is also beneficial that parents seek a relationship with their child that responds to the need of their generation instead of programming them to live the experience they had growing up as a child. When a parent shows a child that they are high on control and support, that child becomes more open and will gradually see their parents' correction as not been punitive but supportive.

How do you demonstrate to your child that you are listening? Sometimes listening becomes difficult when your personal life is filled with noise. As a parent, you could be dealing with the overhead costs, broken dreams, a painful separation, the poor parenting you received and the conflict to appear strong when you tell others about your hurt and failures. These are the parts of you your child cannot perceive because you never allow them to experience the real you. Your child will know you are ready to listen when you validate what they are experiencing through your own personal life experiences. Bringing them to a therapist or merely purchasing them a self-help book is not sufficient to bridge that gap or create an environment that is supportive and healing. When you open up to your children and use your experience to help them navigate their journey, they will know you are connected to their issues, as you crossover to their place of deficit and show them there is more. When you listen, validate, and share, an opening is created for future communication as the child understands that they have your attention.

As children move towards their teenage years, parents are often conflicted with the new behaviors that emerge. Some parents deem the distance they are experiencing with their children as a barrier or even disrespect. The truth is, as young teens go through puberty, they start having issues of their own. They are dealing with insecurities with their body image and how they blend in with the multiple variations of the "perfect teenager" demonstrated by their peers. Oftentimes, teens are battling with depression and show more interest in the opinion of their peers than their parents. This depression could potentially lead to poor performance in school, drug and alcohol use, unsafe sexual practices, and other delinquent behaviors.

One misconception that exist as a child develops is that their parents do not understand what they are experiencing. This is often quite the contrary. Parents do understand; however, it is more about knowing how to relate to the developmental changes, learning compassion and understanding the barriers that exists between them and their child. Listening to students, they perceive their parent's lack of understanding as distance. Although at times your child may be unapproachable and opposes your guidance, leave that open door of support that they can comfortably walk through should they return for help. Sometimes, doing random check-ins can be perceived as being authentic. How often do you sit with your child and asked them about their friends, fears, passion, emotional struggles, and sexual desires or where they are hurting? You will never know if they are ready to talk or need more time unless you meet them where they are instead of trying to bring them to where you are.

The absent parent absent child phenomenon has its roots in parents not spending or having quality time to garner a better understanding of their children. The preoccupation with meeting basic needs sometimes causes the parent to miss out on important opportunities in connecting deeper with their child. One common mistake parents make is thinking that they are losing their children as they get older. Frankly speaking, your child does need that space to develop and become a more independent individual so they can find their place and purpose in this world. The resistance that parents experience, which can be disturbing, is an opportunity for creative contact to be made.

This creative contact is visible when the parent, without being intrusive, builds a supportive community around their child by mobilizing the child's peer arena to support in the areas that the parent feels they are unable to make contact. One parent I worked with in the past incorporated this creative contact by inserting herself in the area her daughter was communicating a need. When her daughter Janice was experiencing social anxiety, the parent asked Janice to provide a list of friends she would like to invite over on weekends. She reached out to Janice's friends and planned fun activities that also involved the family as a whole. This allowed the joy Janice experienced with her friends to spread across the family unit. No matter how old your child gets in life they will always need their parents or wish they were still present in their life when they are gone. As parents, stay focused on being a stable source your child can run to, and no matter what the past was, be ready the meet them in the here and now.

Notes to Parent

- Take time out of your busy schedule to have a heart-to-heart talk with your child.
- Don't be afraid to address uncomfortable topics (sex, drugs, truancy, etc.).
- When your child is ready to talk, listen.
- Your child is not fully mature, so be ready for errors.
- Find time in your schedule to be present with the things they are passionate about.

The Struggle Is Real

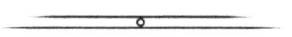

The challenges parents face in raising their children cannot go unnoticed and although it creates some absence from the family unit, they are worth exploring. Every family unit is different and so are the issues. I have worked over the years with single parents whose reality is connected to separation, divorce, mental health challenges and diagnosed illness. These individual circumstances put pressure on the family system and uniquely trigger the absent parent phenomenon. Conversely, there are parents with similar situations yet they are successful in being present with their children amidst challenges. As each home is different, so are the coping mechanisms used to ensure that contact is maintained with each child.

Working with students who are at risk of entering the juvenile system, I often meet with families to get a better understanding of what support is needed in the home. Students with a higher risk of delinquent behaviors are often raised by a single parent. When contact is made to engage these parents in the treatment process, there tends to be some resistance due to these parents not having the flexibility on their jobs to be off work once a week to meet at the school. These parents are torn between maintaining a roof over their heads or be present in the treatment process of their children; they often chose the former. What happens is that the child understands the weaknesses that exist within the family unit and often display rebellious and externalizing behaviors knowing the likelihood of their parent to not intervene.

    As a counselor, when you listen to these parents, they really do have a strong desire of wanting to be there for their child, but they are wrapped up in the pain and bitterness of their lives and why life turned out the way it did for them. I have seen the tears and have heard the cry. These parents are not defending their absence, they are explaining their reasons why. The truth is, children find ways to cope with the absence as they are quick to share that their parent won't be available and are too busy working and have obligations to other siblings in the home or whatever the case may be. Behaviors such as underage drinking, drug use, fights, truancy, destruction of property, and other impulsive behaviors, often uncover a deeper cry for support and advocacy for the pain the child is experiencing. While there is an appreciation for the parent admitting their aloneness with their journey, there must be a collaboration with other support systems within their community so the appropriate help needed can be given. While the parent reconciles their private struggles, greater attention is needed for the developing child to grow up feeling loved and protected.

I recently worked with Lydaas, a single mother of two children diagnosed with autism. When she got frustrated with the behaviors experienced in the home, I would often hear her yell to the high-functioning child, "Call your dad to come and help me, I can't do this alone." One day she apologized for her constant display of weakness of not being able do it alone. She explained that when her husband found out that their first child was diagnosed with autism spectrum disorder (ASD), he became absent from the process and no sooner filed for divorce. She told me that even though the second child had a similar diagnosis, he is more functional and helpful. Lydaas communicated that the high-risk behaviors hampered on the attention needed for the ordinary functioning family members. She shared how difficult it was for her mental health as she oftentimes felt overwhelmed with the guilt of not caring for her children enough. Leaving a mom to raise two children diagnosed with a mental behavioral condition is a breeding ground for absentee parenting, as one child potentially will be underserved.

From my experience working with this family, when decisions are being made that involve therapy at home, community activities or a doctor's appointment, the second child is rescheduled as the parent often lacks the support system to furnish the needs of each child. What goes unmentioned in situations like these is the risk of mental illness that the parent is exposed to. In an effort to maintain her moral obligation to the well-being of her children, the needed personal self-care is sacrificed, creating mental health challenges that could further compromise the welfare of the children that desperately need her support. However, the resilience I saw in this parent and the personal sacrifices she made daily to safeguard the well-being of her children was inspiring. Although she was not able to be fully present, she found her unique rhythm to juggle the needs of raising two teenage boys with autism as a single parent.

I had the privilege of working with another student, Sherika, whose mother had recently been paralyzed due to an unexpected medical condition. This situation impacted the family significantly. Her father had to work longer hours to maintain all the financial needs of the family and the added medical expenses. These changes within the family dynamic created empty places that needed to be filled. Sherika was left to navigate her academic journey on her own as her father's attention was diverted to keeping up with the overwhelming

overhead expenses than keeping a watchful eye over Sherika's academic progress. When I met Sherika in my office, her presenting problem was marijuana use while at school.

As a counselor, my role is to explore beyond the presenting problem to see if the client is at risk for other juvenile delinquent behaviors. Sherika expressed to me that she used marijuana as a coping method to escape the stressors of her living conditions, particularly the instant decline in her mother's health. Sherika was failing classes in school and exhibited chronic truancy and other rebellious and externalizing behaviors towards peers and faculty. As our therapeutic alliance developed, Sherika opened up about her role in assisting her mom before and after school. The absence of her mom and dad was unexpected and created other challenges for her as she resorted to dysfunctional coping mechanisms. The deficiency in her support system was the fuel to the fire that set ablaze an immediate crisis. Sometimes the unexpected happens and as parents, even though the challenge may be out of your control, you can still be present by ensuring your child has an accountability partner, a mentor — someone who will stand in the gap and check in to ensure that your child is not at risk of developing a juvenile record or drop out of school entirely. If you can't be present, your child will know you're still there if you commit them to someone else for oversight and development.

The Involved Parent

Don't be afraid to seek the help from others. It is important as parents that you adopt the "it takes a village to raise a child" mindset. You have to abandon the guilt that makes you feel that you are transferring your responsibility on others and accept that you just cannot do it alone. Sometimes neighbors and friends are ready and waiting to support you but don't want to be intrusive. The truth is both you and your child could benefit immensely from a support system that is non-judgmental and accepting.

Notes to Parent

- Spend some time to take care of yourself to avoid the burn out.
- What you endure will not always be understood, so remain committed to your role as caregiver.
- Never underestimate the effectiveness of having an accountability partner to keep you in line.
- Your child may not want to overwhelm you with the fact that they are aware you are struggling. When they do, be honest.

The "Wow" Moment

We often hear about success stories of perseverance and tenacity that open one up to receive their "wow" moment. The story of Paula, who raised her three boys as a single mother demonstrated practical strategies that can be employed to stay present with your child in the midst of unexpected challenges. When asked how she maintained a balance with all three children, she shared the importance of trusting that good people will help.

Paula did not have the resources or time to be present for her children and their various social and emotional needs. However, she ensured that in every environment they were in, she had a stable adult who would assume responsibility for their care until she arrived. She used the power of trust and collaboration to get her through her most difficult times. Paula spoke about the importance of having a calendar and how effective it was in helping her forecast the engagements her children were to attend. This organization was effective as it helped her to schedule the support she needed. Respecting the time of others and communicating changes and cancellations guided Paula to have consistency in her support network.

Not only did she benefit from the help of others but she and her children would return acts of kindness to those who supported them when she was not able to be physically present. When I asked Paula why she felt a need to do this, she told me that she needed to teach her children the importance of sowing and reaping. She wanted them to know that it is honorable to give back to those who have sown into their lives. She believed that it takes a village to raise a child and when life took an unexpected turn, she went to the available help. Physically, she was not always able to support and be present for her children but she felt they knew she was always there because she connected them to safe people who supported her efforts.

The struggle is indeed real. Perfect conditions don't always produce perfect parents. Sometimes unexpected circumstances will shift you from what once worked perfectly. The challenge now is how as parents you rebound after a loss of a partner, a job, medical crisis, and still be present for your child. The personal stories above show the reality that things can happen to trigger the absent parent phenomenon and affects consciously or subconsciously the family unit. The importance of collaboration and building trusting relationships gives your children a sense of peace, contentment, security, and stability. The risk factors are immense and effective strategies must be sought to ensure that the safety and well-being of your child is a priority as you navigate through unexpected challenges.

Notes to Parent

- Don't be embarrassed to ask for help.
- Teach your children the power of gratitude.
- Communicate with your children on why you can't physically be there.
- Build a trusting relationship with your child.

The Healthy Talk

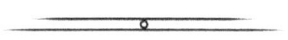

Nothing can take the power from a conversation that evokes personal change. When we are able to comfortably share our hurts, the sooner the healing process begins. There are so many factors that impede the "healthy talk." The truth is we all struggle with something that shifts us from being constantly connected to our ideal self. We have all put on that mask to convince others that we are well but the moment they leave our presence, we realize we lost an opportunity to be real. Working with teens and their parents, it is apparent that mental health challenges are not openly discussed. As young adults begin to navigate the world, hidden traumatic experiences translate into suicidal thoughts, depression, anxiety and other mental health challenges, if they are pushed under the rug. Parents are encouraged to engage age appropriate healthy conversation with their children about their personal challenges. Transparency is important when working with adolescents. They are already gathering information about life from their peer arena. It is incumbent on the parent to re-author any misleading narrative by appropriately sharing personal stories or experiences so their truth will resonate with their children.

The discomfort some parents feel about having conversations about sex with teenagers exposes them to an even higher level of risk. The truth is the brain is not completely developed until the age of 25 and the child is not fully equipped to make rational decisions during this stage of their lives. The tendency to exercise poor judgment, creates a deeper need for adult guidance and monitoring. The sad truth is, some teenagers only begin to embrace safe sexual practices after they have been infected with a sexually transmitted disease (STD) or unexpected pregnancy.

I had a client who in his first sexual encounter contracted genital herpes. This was discovered when he saw breakout of rashes on his genitalia. Jason shared with me how wrecked he was when he found out the news at a local clinic. He reports how fearful he was to communicate this news to anyone. Jason was devastated and became even more distant from his parents. He refused to share the information as he felt they would isolate themselves and blame him for being irresponsible. He states that his mom and dad always warned him about safe sex practices but he felt like he needed to figure the world out on his

own terms. This is the typical mindset of teenagers. Although Jason's life was not about to be cut short, he knew that a lot was about to change. He knew he was a carrier of a STD for which there was no cure. He also understood that this condition will remain with him for the rest of his life. In his future relationships, he would have to explain this disease so others are not infected without consent.

As my sessions continued with Jason, whenever we discussed communicating his health condition to his parents, he firmly noted that he was 18 and could handle his own problems. He believed that he had disappointed his parents tremendously and didn't want to create "unnecessary" distraction or attention. He knew once the news about his illness was revealed to his parents, he would face severe backlash and rejection. Jason felt his revelation would bring shame to the family and distract his parents from their professional life. He didn't want his parents to treat him like a child and constantly remind him of how much he inherited the consequence of his disobedience. Jason thought that the high expectations his parents set for him were now unattainable. I provided Jason a list of support groups he could attend to connect with people with similar illnesses; he rejected. The great irony in this counseling relationship was that Jason was not ashamed to express his emotions and concerns. His desire to connect with a trusted peer created anxiety as he felt the closer he got to someone, the deeper his guilt in not being able to be completely honest. Jason made a choice to preserve the family image at the expense of the emotional support he desperately needed.

The absent parent emerges when there are high expectations without accommodation for errors. A child needs to know that home will be the first place of rescue, that is judgment free. This provides the family unit an opportunity to support each other or seek professional help. If a child does not feel safe communicating to their parent's life altering changes, the higher the potential is for them to be engaged in self-destructive behaviors. Teenagers need to know that no matter how they failed or have failed your expectations, your relationship with them is what matters most. The open-door policy needs to be embedded in every family unit so communication can be transparent and authentic. The solution focused approach needs to be embraced when working with teenagers. When presented with information from your children that is in conflict with the value system of the family, values must be reinforced but a solution to the problem must also be explored. If your reaction is rejection when your child discloses their private errors, you could lose their trust forever. Instead, explore meaningful solutions to your child's needs so healing could take place and the oppression of guilt and aloneness be expelled from their environment. The issue was not whether

Jason felt loved, he felt like he had to preserve family values over his personal victory. For Jason, he was experiencing victory personally because although he knew he had a medical condition that would impact his overall health, he was coping inwardly with the consequences of his own decision. Taking responsibility for his actions allowed him to embrace the healing process. Jason was winning from within and wished he could take his personal victory outward.

The healthy talk is necessary for teens to have with their parents and conversely for parents to have with their teens. As a mental health professional, what has been consistent is that the majority of the teenagers I worked with had a parent or close family member living with a mental health condition. These students knew the medical terminology and medication that they used for treatment. This explains just how connected teens are with the presence of mental illness in their environment and their openness to be educated. Sometimes out of fear parents hide their mental health challenges from their children to preserve their strength, influence and effectiveness in the family unit.

For years, Tori struggled to understand what was happening with her mother. Her mom had severe mood swings and lacked interest in pleasurable activities. These affected Tori

significantly as she was involved in team sports and her mom would never show up to support her. Her mother blamed her absence on working late. Although Tori adjusted to the absence of her mom, there were other behaviors that had her attention; her mother's weight loss. Tori began noticing that her mom hardly ate, even after she prepared dinner for her and her brother. She recalled one day asking her mom about her eating habits and mom's response was that she was on a diet. There were moments when her mom would forget important appointments and school events; Tori reported that she had adjusted to her mom's tendency to be absent.

While working with Tori, she asked if I was willing to reach out with her mom and check-in to see if she was doing well. Clinically, I had an inclination of what was going on with her mom, but I wanted this opportunity to engage and not force my way into the family unit. The following day, I reached out to her mom to introduce myself and offered my support in helping her as I supported Tori. The conversation took an interesting turn. She began to pour out her private struggle with depression. She shared that ever since her husband passed, life for her had never been the same. Medically, she reported that her condition has worsened and she relied heavily on medication to regulate her emotions. The touching part of our conversation was that she felt a need to protect Tori from this private struggle because she did not want Tori to think she was losing her. This story is common among many households; Tori was suffering from the symptoms of her mom's diagnosis. The more absent the parent became the more absent the child.

Tori agreed to have her mom attend one of our sessions. I used the opportunity to facilitate open discussions about the behaviors she reported her mom frequently displayed. In addition, I supported her mother as she disclosed to her daughter the reality behind her actions. As the mom shared with Tori what she was experiencing medically, both broke down in tears. Tori shared with her mom how open and receptive she would have been toward her had she known about her private issues. They both apologized for their absent behavior and are now on a path to repair their broken communication and to become more supportive of each other's needs. Diagnosis within a family unit does affect most, if not all participants vicariously. When age appropriate, the child involved should learn about it so the cognitive adjustment can begin. Ignoring the importance of having the healthy talk with your child when you need support creates the absent parent absent child phenomenon.

While acknowledging personal challenges, the overall goal for you as a parent, is to experience wholeness and move on to live a meaningful life with your child. A quality conversation about physical and emotional health must be had to ensure that the outcome is positive. Parents must leave room for error as their child develops no matter what standards you require them to maintain. The truth is, your child's brain is still not fully developed and errors are inevitable. One way a parent can be more present is by leaving the door open for your child to walk through and discuss where they are failing or need support. Adolescents often appear to be emotionally tough when they put up a resistance to change. However, as long as they know support and a helping hand is available, they will engage and share more. When facing any medical condition or set back, the first place to start is with open conversation. Ignoring social and emotional health can trigger lifetime of pain and resentment when real problems emerge. Overall, we are all being challenged by something and are all at different level of readiness to make change. The next move is on you!

Notes to Parent

- Embrace an open environment where authentic communication can occur.
- Don't not allow embarrassment to destroy a collaborative and supportive environment.
- Always have checkpoints where talk about health can occur.
- Make your home a safe place for your child.
- There needs to be a judgment-free zone so information is not withheld to preserve personal or family image.

Words are Arrows

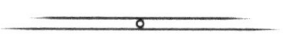

Even if you are absent, your words are always present. This must be the guiding light to every relationship. When a negative or discouraging word leaves one's mouth, the impact is still felt when you have left the physical space in which it was spoken. Even if an apology is given, the impact it has on the person to whom it was spoken to cannot be retracted. Words are like an arrow seeking a target and when landed successfully will leave a scar or positive impact when the arrow is removed. As we continue this dialogue about the absent parent absent child phenomenon, it must be understood that the words we speak must aim to inspire, ignite, and uplift. I have observed many conversations with students and their parents, and when they leave the room, I often wonder how they will reconcile their differences after all they have just shot at each other. What happens if reconciliation never takes place before parent and child part ways in adulthood? Both child and parent are left with a scar that can negatively affect future relationships.

Is it true that hurt people, hurt people? Yes! When an individual is emotionally overloaded or experiencing life stressors, such pressure compromises one's ability to monitor the emotions their words may carry. The agenda here is not to discredit parenting styles or to change the culture of communication within families but to foster a better understanding of how one functional environment can be dysfunctional to another. I previously worked with a teenager who said it was "normal" for his parents to curse at him and each other in their house. He thought the way his parents communicated was normal, until one day his father told him to give up on the dreams to attend college as his academics weren't good enough. Past communications within the family unit seemed normal but that conversation impacted him in a personal way. Those words triggered depression, anxiety, low self-esteem, and bitterness towards his father. Additionally, he began to experience the early onset of agoraphobia (perceiving the outside world and its environment as an unsafe place).

It is important that the words used in time of anger towards your children does not block them from seeking out other support in their environment. When children who are looking to their parents for social and emotional development hear they are a failure, they struggle at times to find other willing adults support as genuine; fearing a repeat of their prior ordeal in their family unit. I always encourage parents I work with to use their words wisely. Remember, your kids are young and need more support and guidance from you than they can advocate for themselves. A moment of uncontrolled rage can destroy a future bond as the child sometimes holds on to the hurt for a long time. As we bridge the gap between parent and child, it is important to communicate respectfully on both ends of the conversation, so healing replaces pain and acceptance replaces being judgmental.

Our words are either healing or wounding.

During our sessions, I could feel the presence of the transference this young man was experiencing. He had difficulty at times being receptive to treatment with me being a compassionate male in his life could seemingly be perceived as being disingenuous. I had to incrementally build his trust to become receptive to therapy and begin the journey of re-authoring his story to a life of happiness with infinite possibilities. When hurtful words are internalized, they can lead the individual to accept their intent as a true reflection of who they will become. This was the challenge in the treatment process. This student had accepted all his dad's words as truth

and used his actions to defend dad's words. Whenever he would fail in school, he would see truth in his dad's prediction of him not being better than going to a 2-year college or not being smart enough to be a doctor. During our sessions, a phrase that was on repeat was, "Maybe he's right." While continuing to work with this student, I could not help but wonder about the person he would be today if those negative affirmations were not spoken over his life.

    As a parent there is a need to monitor the words we speak to our children; they could still be living in your house but totally absent from your presence. It is no easy task raising a child or even grooming a teenager. However, your quest to maintain the role of adult cannot be achieved at the expense of your child's social and emotional development. Your words shape the person they become. Your house must be a home and not a holding center. There needs to be ongoing personal assessment on how parent and child interaction occurs, with the understanding that what works in your house is not universal. Someday your child will evaluate where they have been and how much they accepted as the norm what the wider society rejects. As simple as calling your child "stupid" may sound to you, it means so much more to your child than you could imagine. They use your words to evaluate the words of others. The sad truth is sometimes even when other people try to help repair the wounds your words have created, there are those who are so torn that healing is just a concept and the pain is their reality. Let us not project our pain on them. No matter the challenges you face raising your child, even if they need to learn from their mistakes, speak well over their journey and always leave the door open for positive communication.

Notes to Parent

- Once you say something, you can't take it back.
- Know when to walk away when you are upset as hurting people hurt people.
- You are never too old or too young to apologize.
- Let your words make others better and not bitter.

The Honor Code

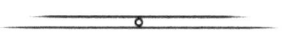

As children develop and gain more independence, respect and honor must be the fundamental principles that guide their existence. One of the greatest challenges parents face in grooming their children is making them receptive to guidance. Children are more apt to follow the guidance from teachers, coaches and mentors but seldom assume a posture of respect in listening to their parents. When a farmer goes to his field to nurture his seed, the seed is receptive to the fertilizer that is being used to help it grow. One of the challenges of this fast-moving generation is seeing life as a learning journey and not a sprint race. Something I have seen in my profession is parents crying in my presence when their child is booked for jail or in trouble with the law. Another popular cry I've heard from parents is, "I told him but he did not listen." This reality is frequent in the absent parent absent child phenomenon. The challenges parents face dealing with the absence of their children to the justice system is unbearable. What do you do when your words of positive redirection are met with rejection and your tears cannot bring your absent child home? As a parent you still have to be present. Your child may have hit a pothole in life and needs you to be that repair shop to fix what is seemingly damaged.

    Monica shared her personal story of the moment the police came to her house and handcuffed her son. She recalls the multiple times she offered support and recommended help with his anger issues. Merrick was charged with assault after being involved in a fight with his girlfriend. Monica's initial response was that she did all she could and that maybe this was the only way he will learn. No matter what mistake your child has made they are still looking for you to show up and be that shoulder they can lean on in difficult times. Monica abandoned her anger towards Merrick and sought immediate legal assistance for his release from jail. When he came out she had a conversation with him about how she felt about the whole situation but restate her intent to support his social and emotional recovery. Both parent and child partnered together on this journey. Today, Monica and her husband assisted Merrick in opening his own business and his behaviors have reduced dramatically. This is a classic example of the involved parent. No matter what your child has done or how they made you feel, be present; in their most difficult times they are still looking for you to show up.

When working with teenagers, they attribute the breakdown in communication with their parents to their lack of understanding that the times have changed. Seemingly, teens and young adults have concluded that their parents are out of touch with their reality. While it is true that the trends have changed over the years, disrespect to what was cannot be the ground where the "new you grows." The change in times is an opportunity for both parent and child to sit at the table in a calm manner and accept the knowledge that both bring to the table. Some degree of patience is needed for the information to be processed and for acceptance to be the sign of change. What I have gathered from parents as I explore this area within the family unit, is that the children are demanding instant change and allowing the outer society to dictate their value system and change the rules that are embedded in the family structure. The majority of the parents I have interviewed are open and accepting of things that are changing but their children must understand that the purpose of guardianship is to protect. Recently, one mother said to me, "If the brain is fully developed at 25, why should I think my child at the age 15 can assume the responsibility of his own safety?" Beyond cultural differences and change in trends, as your child develops and naturally finds their own place in this world, and never forgets that the respect you want them to convey to you must be taught regardless of the push back they display. If children hear your screams and curses above solid reasoning, that's what they are going to accept as normal and translate it in other areas of their lives.

I believe experiential learning is impactful and transformative. Some people do need to learn from their mistakes and others learn from the mistake of others. Raul was being raised by parents who were almost 40 years older than his current age. He was always saying that his parents are too old to understand his needs. Raul would communicate with hurtful words, "You guys are old people," "I wish I had younger parents," the list goes on. These words are painful for any parent to hear from a child they are nurturing. The more they demanded respect, the more hurtful the words became. Raul's mom told me that one of the toughest decisions she and her husband made was to accept that they may have to prepare for a time to come when they will have to help him clean the self-inflicted wounds and heal. When parental guidance is ignored by children, they are communicating that they'd rather learn from their own mistakes. Their efforts to do life as they know it and abandon the guidance of those who have gone before speaks to their personal acceptance of the outcome. After dealing with aggressive and dismissive behaviors from Raul, they were greeted at 1:00 am one morning by the local police officers with a warrant for Raul's arrest. He was being charged with domestic violence with serious bodily harm. Both parents watched their son who resisted their guidance walked away in handcuffs. Is it possible that their old age provided them with wisdom to predict what was ahead? Could the guidance that seemed annoying be their attempt to shield Raul from areas in life where they failed?

After one year of court appearances and expensive legal fees, Raul's parents are in debt to a reality that they tried so hard to avoid. Some will argue that this was a necessary learning, but how many parents today are living in pain and in debt while lawyers and probation officers are telling their children the very lessons they were trying to teach them at home. There were many times Raul's parents would encourage him to get home early, watch for the friends he spent time with, get help for his anger issues, and stop doing drugs. All these things were met with resistance and he branded them as being out of touch with his needs. Today, Raul has a criminal record, lost his job and is now struggling to provide for the welfare of his newborn child. Additionally, the law requires him to attend anger management classes for six months and check-in weekly with his probation officer. Now he has to stop and listen to the information that his parents were providing all along. Raul returned to his parent's home and is learning from them the guiding principles to

rebound from his mistakes. Even though his hurtful words pushed them away, they kept the door of love wide open.

This statement holds truth: "Even in our absence, our words are present." There needs to be more thought in how parents and children negotiate their roles and independence in the family unit. In an age where we are triggered by social media to say what is on our minds, many learned this is not the best way to live even in a modern world. When we release an arrow of negative fighting words, we cannot run and take it back. Therefore, both parent and child must consider the irreversible consequence of their words. Let's move from contradiction and leave patience in the midst as the mediator.

Notes to Parent

- Even when your child does the opposite of what you have taught them, still be present and support their recovery.
- Feel comfortable restating your position while opening the door for support.
- Comfortably share with your child where you made mistake or have learned from the mistakes of others.
- Believe your child can be better and point them to those resources that can improve their lives.

How to Be More Present

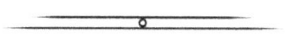

The dialogue about the absent parent and the absent child is aimed at answering one central question: as a parent, how do you remain more present with your child? There will inevitably be challenges that both parent and child face privately that create distance. However, having the right tools and strategies can avert a lifetime of pain for the family as a unit. Separation on any level carries its own unique level of distress; everyone handles pain differently. What is also effective is knowing how to communicate your feelings so that your voice is heard and the absence you experience is not self-inflicted. Being present with your child is not limited to physical environment, it is also providing an atmosphere where you can be touched. When a child knows they can fearlessly articulate their concerns to their parent, the risk of self-inflicted wounds is reduced and functional help becomes available. The parent needs to display a level of honesty, not putting their challenges above the needs of their children. These tools and strategies will only work when parental power and authority does not get in the way of vulnerability and openness.

The Sandwich Approach

Give positive feedback

Provide constructive criticism

Give positive feedback

One of the greater challenges you will face as a parent is not what to say but how you communicate your intentions appropriately to safeguard a lasting relationship with your child. The power dynamic of parent over child naturally creates resistance and blocks future opportunities of having productive conversation. Sometimes it is much easier for parents to say how they feel because they are the authority in the house and the child depends on them for support and survival. What I have discovered over the years of mentoring and counseling is that children are archiving these hurtful comments and gradually use them to form a more permanent reflection of who their parents are at their core. This reasoning they adapt is not always reflective of who their parents really are but what they say out of anger or in a heated moment. The Sandwich approach when used is very effective in being intentional about your message in a non-offensive manner; with the end goal of preserving relationships.

The Compliment: "The first layer of bread"

This approach works great in all areas of one's personal life. In the context of this book, when communicating with teens, seek out praise for something good the child has done before the negative reprimand surfaces. The focus on the positive, signals acknowledgement that a supportive environment exists and forms the pillow where parental correction rest.

Scenario: You are dealing with a teenage child who refuses to clean his room which creates an uncomfortable smell in the house.

Example: Jordan, I just want you to know I am proud of your efforts in being responsible by making sure the garbage is taken out every day this week.

This compliment may be hard to produce when your anger and tolerance as a parent has reached its maximum. However, what this framework does is set an atmosphere for the child to be receptive and better handle the incoming criticism. People are generally more receptive to compliments than criticisms. The Sandwich approach validates the effectiveness of accepting both as beneficial to the human development. What tends to happen in instances where parent and child engage in verbal battle is that the conversation goes unfiltered and the negativity released can make a later apology seem disingenuous. It is important for parents to let their positive affirmations precede any criticism so their child can know their intent is not to look down at their faults but lift them to a higher place.

The Criticism: "The meat of the matter"

It is very important for parents at this level of interaction to focus the criticism on the behavior and not the person. This allows the child not to feel targeted but supported in accomplishing your desired expectation. The overall goal is not to try and change the person but to change their behavior. One mistake parents make is comparing their child's weaknesses to the strength of other peers known of their child. This is often done in an attempt to reinforce the conviction. This strategy is not as effective as you think. It has the potential of escalating your child's insecurity. When you are using this approach focus on your child and the facts, so they are energized to make the needed change you are highlighting for their personal success.

Example: Jordan, although you did a great job with the garbage, if you don't practice doing a better job cleaning your room the smell is going to escalate. Hearing your friends complain about this when they come over will make me look bad.

The parent has focused on the facts about the room and its condition, with the behavior being the primary focus. The parent was clear and concise in how they felt and kept it very respectful. When this approach is implemented, the relationship with parent and child is left intact. The parent validated how she felt but never let her feelings be the focus of the conversation. The change in Jordan's behavior was her target. Sometimes it is difficult to deliver negative information. With this approach, the foundation is laid for support at the first layer of bread and even after the criticism is given in the middle, the second layer of bread will maintain a positive outlook on the individual outside their behavior. It is also a good way of teaching your child to accept criticism and also communicate them to others in a non-offensive manner.

The Compliment: "Second layer of bread"

This layer is where the parent gets an opportunity to communicate with the child that there is genuine connectedness beyond the "meat of the matter." The parent can restate the initial positive feedback, address the improvement observed, and appreciate the child's acceptance of the criticism made.

Example: Jordan, you are a very responsible person and I know getting your room tidy will be something else to add to the other great things you're doing. I appreciate you for being so receptive to my observation.

This is the sandwich approach, when used accurately, it serves as a tool to de-escalate tense conversations and preserve relationships. Ending any conversation with a positive tone shows some level of openness to the person and acknowledgment of their feelings. Parents sometimes forget to focus on the feelings their words carry when talking to their child. It is very important that after having this quality conversation with your child, they see that you still care and support their journey to the desired change.

Notes to Parent

- It is not what you say but how you say it.
- Ensure that after you have criticized your child, you reaffirm their strengths.
- How you feel is valid but focus on the facts of the behavior.
- Remember the behavior is what you are trying to change and not your child.
- Each person is unique so be careful not to compare your child with other.

What Box Are You In?

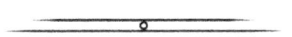

The social discipline window offers parents a guide to effectively engage their children in a manner that is restorative and supportive. This framework supports the restorative practice fundamental principle, which believes that as humans we experience more joy, are more engaged and resourceful, and make positive change in behaviors when those in places of power do things with them, rather than to them or for them.

The TO Box: Here, parents rely more on the punitive approach. Punitive approaches are when parents use punishment to resolve an act of indiscipline done by their child. These acts include withdrawal of privileges, loss of prized possessions and time out. They are high on limits and expectation and low on support; increasing pressure to conform in lieu of consequence. Frankly speaking, the parents sets the rule and if broken, the child is at threat of isolation, loss of resources, punishment and privilege. This parenting approach has the potential to produce a child who could develop anger, feelings of resentment, guilt shame and disempowerment. This authoritarian role is stigmatizing and never allows the parent and child to genuinely connect.

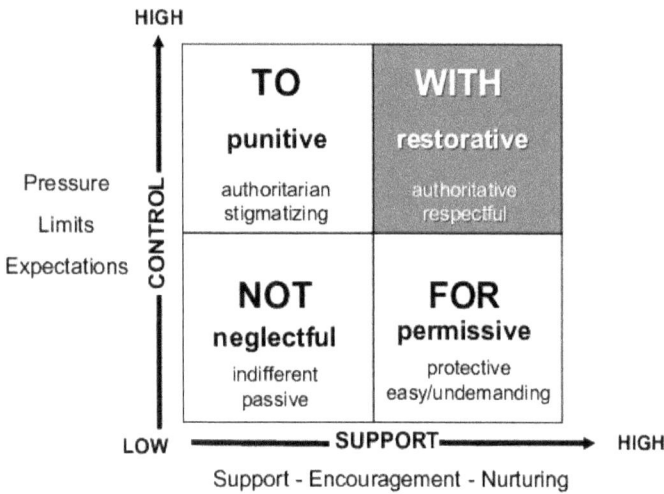

The NOT Box: In this box the parent is absent, sometimes physically, mentally, and emotionally. There is low expectation of the child by the parent and low support of the parent towards the needs of the child. In the "NOT" box the parent has no expectations, no consequences, no rules or guidelines. This lack of support and structure has the potential of fostering the development of a child who struggles with fears, loneliness and disengagement. When a parent becomes distant, the attention the child desires can potentially be occupied by others that point them to juvenile delinquent behaviors. This box should be totally avoided by parents. No matter what the situation is with you and your child, always leave the door open for restoration.

The FOR Box: In this parenting environment the rules are always evolving. The lack of structure creates instability and children typically chose which rules to obey and when. The parents are low on control and high on support. What typically happens is, the parent's life constantly revolves around the needs of the child. This level of support and parent engagement delays the development of executive functioning skills. When the child displays inappropriate behaviors, the parents verbalize consequences but they are never executed. Parents, when your child goes out in the wider society they will encounter a different level of support, where independence is expected. When the child does not meet developmental milestones due to over supportive parenting, the response is often fear, apathy, distrust, low motivation, and low self-esteem.

The WITH Box: This box is where most parents are encouraged to be as they foster the development of their children. As a parent you want to have high control and high support. This approach results in a more restorative and collaborative environment. In the WITH box, rules and expectations are clear and any deviation is immediately corrected. In these situations, the parent restates the expected behavior using emotive statements to reinforce real world consequences to action. In this collaborative environment where expectations are consistent and clear, the child develops a natural ability to be collaborative, creative, autonomous, empowered, and engage. This is possible because the child is being supported and embraces correction when behaviors conflict established norms.

Notes to Parent

- The greatest act of authority is showing support to your child after you set boundaries.
- If the rules are always changing then so will your child behaviors.
- Neglecting your child because of their behavior leave them open to delinquent behaviors due to lack of guidance.
- Having high control and high support will build longer lasting relationships.

Pulling It Together

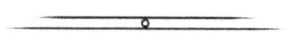

In today's busy world, it becomes challenging for parents to find meaningful time to take care of their children in an expressive way. The truth is, if you are not available to yourself, it's hard to be available to anyone else. Even though you may be present in the house with your child, it does not mean you are available to them. Oftentimes, parents who are overworked experience fatigue which deprive them of the energy to support the needs of their children. Sometimes as a parent, you have to stop and ask the question, "Am I really available?" If your honest answer is, "No," you are not alone and you are also at a great place where existential change can now begin.

One parent I worked with infused self-care as a family moment. He struggled for years to maintain a connection with his daughters due to his hectic work schedule. He designed a plan to remain present with his children amidst his busy roster. He one day sat down and asked his children to make a list of things they would love to do with him being there. Initially, he was nervous but was open to try to do the uncomfortable. He then asked his wife to make a list of things she would want to do with him alone. What he found out was that they all had some identical items on their individual lists. He learned that they wanted to do activities as a family — together. They designed a strategy to complete all the identical events on summer vacations and do one from each list monthly. This was the tool they used to remain more connected and healthier as a family unit.

The truth is everyone in the family has a unique need. Studies have shown that parents who have a closer connection with their children see less juvenile delinquent behavior. When the unit functions as a whole, conversations become easy and no one is left feeling underappreciated. To have a close relationship with your teenage child, you cannot be a distant parent. You have to put in the work, push indelicately against the developmental isolation, affirm your open-door policy, validate strengths and invest in weakness and insecurities. If your child cannot approach you to talk, best believe they are already talking to someone else. While you hold firm your authority as the adult in the room, never forget the child that was in you and that someone was patient with your process as you developed and grew to who you are today. Now, go ahead and do something with your child that you have not done in a while.

Notes to Parent

- You are not alone with the struggle of being more involved with your child.
- Use strategies that fit the availability and budget of your family; just don't do nothing.
- Be open to help from others.
- Find sometime in the midst of all you do to take care of yourself.

Conclusion

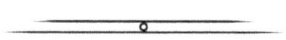

Being and involved parent can be challenging especially living in today's fast paced environment. Parents are overbooked and overworked and often children are left to navigate life as they know it. The hope is that each parent would evaluate their level of contact with their children and utilize the tips and strategies offered to rebuild relationships that are broken and maintain those that are working. *The Involved Parent* is not aimed at judging the efforts of parents in raising their children but provide strategies to remain more connected and supportive.

I have seen lives transformed when parents make the necessary arrangements and restructure their schedule for a greater connection with their child. I helped to coordinate several events where both parent and child could bond. Whether it's a field trip, an award ceremony, parent teacher conference, movie night, or a graduation ceremony. I have always sought opportunities to applaud parents who show up for their children at these moments. I believe that parents too need that extra boost of empowerment for the role they play in the life of their children. Sometimes even the most involved parents feel they are not doing enough for their child and any encouragement will serve as a boost in their effort to continue covering their personal growth.

For those parents who desire to be more involved but lack the resources to be more present, this book encourages the use of available support systems in the community. Should there be any conflict in school or at home surrounding their child, the communication should model the sandwich approach previously explained. I believe all must be open to understand the challenges of the uninvolved parent, boost their efforts in accessing any resources in the community to ensure that they are not left alone with the burden of not being more present. These efforts will continue to improve the level of engagement and energize parents to be more involved.

As I continue to support teens and their families, I endeavor to advocate for better parent and child engagement. The result of having an involved parent is consistent; the child develops with more stability and security as they navigate an independent life. Although engaging the family to sit around one table is challenging, I will continue to utilize my session times to build up the confidence of teens in embracing the collaborative process. I understand how awkward it can be for teenagers to instantaneously open up with their parents. Therefore, as a counselor, I will continue to support the teens with the skills to handle the emotions that will be present in the room and how to respectfully communicate their feelings with their parents being present.

Additionally, I have seen first-hand how this mediation process works successfully. When parents show up for sessions, they often expect a combative environment with their child due to their authority in the room. What always changes the temperature in the room is how respectfully the child is able to express their emotions to their parents. When the parents listen in, they often embrace, apologize or express need for deeper connection. The child feels more accepted and relationship building is initiated.

Cultural competence is important in working with parents and their teens. As I continue to support parent and child to redevelop a stronger bond it is important to understand cultural norms. As a counselor, I must research and accept cultural norms for each family I support. It is very important to support both parent and child through their cultural lens. I see more embrace and openness to family counseling when parents feel they are being supported than judged for doing something wrong. Some cultures are more open to counseling than others. I have seen how supportive efforts have proven more successful than telling parents they are absent. The uninvolved parent sometimes is embarrassed to ask for support because they are raised culturally to resolve issues within the family unit and not seek outside help.

When parent and child can collaborate and respect each other's position; the future of that relationship is preserved. The more engaged parents are with their children the better they will be able to provide the information their child need to avert juvenile delinquent behaviors. The involved parent is not present to only be in control, but rather that safe haven for their child. This is beneficial as the developing child has that pool of knowledge to consult that will guide him/her in the right direction. The opposite of this is the child depending on the inexperience peer to provide guidance. This is what the involved parent secures; a place where information shared is aimed at personal development. The involved parent is necessary to the child's social and emotional development. No matter what behavioral issues your child exhibits, leaving them to navigate this journey alone has continually proven to trigger gaps in development.

Society benefits tremendously when a parent is more involved. From my professional experience, the students whom I supported have one thing in common—an uninvolved parent. The lack of support leaves that child to navigate a journey on their own; they have limited knowledge of what is ahead. When I examine students who decline continually in their academic performance and those who are consistently cutting classes in school, their parent are often not monitoring their attendance records to ensure their child is doing what they should be doing in school. What tends to happen is that the parent becomes reactive when the child is at danger of not graduating or dropping out of school. When parents are more involved, the child has support on their academic journey. The involved parent gets an opportunity to seek out relevant intervention for their child to achieve their best outcome. Society benefits as the child is given support to become successful as oppose to resorting to delinquent behaviors as a response to failure and lack of support.

    The social and emotional development of a child rests heavily on the connection that child has with their parent. A child who has a healthy relationship with their parent, is more confident and secure. This stems from the support received and the guidance provided to correct the behaviors that are delinquent. Supportive parenting builds a community around the child to ensure that during the instances where they can't be present, the child will have help, ensuring normal development is not compromised. Living in an environment where the child looks to authority figures for guidance, ultimately benefits the child's overall success in life as they are able to access knowledge in real time to deal with their personal challenges.

Finally, *The Involved Parent* encourages parents to step outside their generational experience and explore a relationship with their child in the now, accepting them in the framework of their experience. Oftentimes, parents desire to raise their child from the way they grew up. Some values are indeed necessary to be transferred but there needs to be an accommodation and openness to what your child is experiencing in their generation. Most conflicts arise with parent and child because the child feels ignored and pressured to live in a lifetime they never experienced. Your child needs your support and guidance. If you feel overwhelmed, out of touch, or just tired, seek advice and support from others that you know and trust. It sometimes does take a village to raise a child. I encourage you to continue your great work as you support your child to be a change agent in this world.

NOTES

NOTES

NOTES

NOTES

NOTES

NOTES

NOTES

NOTES

NOTES

NOTES

NOTES

NOTES

NOTES

NOTES

NOTES

NOTES

NOTES